# Verses

MW00475045

## by Salvin Chahal

ISBN-13: 978-1499784985
ISBN-10: 1499784988

Cover Designed by Rupy Kaloti

*This is dedicated
to those who have provided me peace
and to those who have disturbed it*

# Table of Contents

# Introduction

While a young man was cleaning his light green room, an oil-based paperback notebook reached out for his arms. It shook his hands for as long as he can remember with the tightest grip he has ever felt. He opened the first page and it asked him, "Do you remember me, we used to be so close, what happened?" Suddenly he was reminded of everything his fingers used to grow towards; friendships that would find a way to fade, women with weird and mysterious personas, and poetry that would rejuvenate the wrinkles in his soul. Each page stood out like a figure in the distance. Before he closed the book, pages flew out of his hands and the words detached themselves to create a forest in his bedroom. He ran towards trees where fruits would drip from and hid from noises that would sound closer in every direction he stepped towards. He lost himself in these woods for twenty years. He would climb branches and carve poetry in the bark. Shavings would fall from the sky and his feet would sing with the soil. Every night he would sleep at the apex of the forest, just so he can rest above everything that was holding him down. One morning, his eyes wandered and found smoke behind the mountains. At that moment, he realized he wasn't alone in the forest anymore.

*These are the verses from above,*

# Travelling man

I have wandered the woods to find you
they say that's where you live

I've travelled all over the world for your love
and did not find you

One night you suddenly appeared like a
shooting star when I rarely visualized the sky

Oh how far have I travelled to meet you

I have touched the ends of this earth in
search of your compassion

I have sacrificed for your love and never
expected your tenderness

I have lost my peers and asked you why do
you commit these unreliable acts

My knees have met many floors many times
and my heart has reconstructed itself even
more

I have left my home in search of you when
you were with me all along

# Try To Find Home

Let the following poems from this book
provide you comfort like the sheets from
home after a tiring vacation

Find a family of words that will raise your
youth

Let the number of pages become directions to
places you hardly find heaven in

# The Wrong Way

She did everything the wrong way
She ran towards problems
She never danced in the rain
She grew up with a father who drank trips to
the hospital every night
He used his unemployed hands on her
daughter for 18 years
And now
Every moment her spouse would use his fists
he would make sure every hit would feel like
home
Every night she would talk to the heavens as
if God is a stranger
Every morning she drops to her knees and
prays that her future
Her gift
Her son
Will not ever end up like her father

# 4:56 am

My hands slither across this paper as my bite
for rest begins to shed

Where do I begin

This year has been full of sunshine like no
other

As well as wickedness unlike before

I have wore tenderness at the edge of my
shoulders

And learned how to wake up without it

All I hope for is

That I won't be saying this again next year

# STORM

I never believed in calm before the storm

Tranquility became my excitement

The sound of the storm can sometimes
silence the anguished

Just like puddles of water

Memories evaporate and then transform
into the shape of clouds

To a land uncharted by the raindrops
of my quondam mind

To someday return and flood on the storm
I've already accustomed myself to

# San Francisco

I caught the bus once to explore a city I have
visited numerous times

Only one seat was available and it was next to
the window

In a matter of seconds this bus turned into a
home for beggars and businessmen

Where they would travel through golden gate
park all the way to the financial district

The smell of each avenue would sting the
back of everyone's lung

As the aroma would remind each one of a
different memory

This moving home became full of poets who
would tell stories of lost love and how
insignificant skyscrapers appeared next to
the sun

Suits gave up seats for street performers

Everyone standing held on to the straps in a

way that made you feel like it was the only
thing they knew how to hold right

And I swear

At that moment

I couldn't tell who was the beggar
and who was the businessman

# Thoughts Before The Approach

I'm writing this piece hoping you and I don't fall into pieces like your heart that you refuse to rescue.

See I barely know you but your eyes scream the story of sadness.

I can't stand that.

So give me time and I'll let you find refugee in my arms and connect the lines in our palms that pave true happiness.

For every frown I foreshadow I see a smile that only I can sustain.

For every smile from every remark that I make, your teeth scars my brain just so I can feel the outlines of our future

Together.

All this and I don't even know your last name.

But I do know how you hate feet, spit and
what you do when you're nervous.

You've been on too many dates with cats that
share characteristics of their fathers.

You can come over and we can scrabble
around so I can play with your words or

We can stay up all night and talk about some
sentimental shit if you want.

*Introduce yourself to anybody and
everybody, you never know what they might
or might not mean to you*

# The Moment

Which would you remember

The moment one takes their breath for the first time

Or the sound of one taking their breath for the last time

# My Sister Is Not A Museum

My sister has history in her bones

She flaunts her flaws like an exhibit knowing
they will one day become prehistoric

She curates herself in a manner that an
infinite amount of wax cannot sculpt

She does not need a tour guide to constantly
tell you that you do not get to touch her

One day someone will take her home

But today she will tell you that pop up shops
are not in her budget because she can't afford
someone who is available for a short period of
time

My sister is not a souvenir you take home
and display somewhere in your living room

Yes, she is a sight to see but not a museum
you visit like a field trip. Don't think you can
enter her foreign land and use her for her
resources the way America does

# Why The Sun Misses The Moon

The sun wrote the moon a poem once and
ripped it into thirty pieces

Hoping it would take her a month to piece
together the promises he's been breaking for
billions of years

He was the center of attention

Everything revolved around him

And she

She was afraid to get hurt if she got any
closer

She only reveals one side of her

Many men have stepped on her surface
which is why she has become a blue moon on
a daily basis

Similar in many ways but the difference was
the distance

Every morning he wishes that he could forget
her name and the fact she ever existed

Move on but know this


*You can always see the moon in the sky*
*wherever the sun seems to shine*

# Planet Z

The majority of inhabitants were destroying their own planet many years ago

They were built on unfiltered education and oceans that consisted of materialistic intent

An atmosphere that was murdered by every factory and car ride to their favorite shopping mall

A planet was discovered that ensured the reset button for every regret that was made

Planet Z is what they called it

They developed the technology to send low class working families of souls to Planet Z

Families that would start over and build this planet from the ground up

Over the years the backbone of their former planet developed a form of diverse art, culture, and activism on Z

Medical facilities were built, and educational institutions were built

Neighborhoods were built but relationships were ruined

They were inhabitants of this planet for so long they lost connection with their mother planet

Living a preoccupied life that consisted of greed, envy and lust

Every day they questioned their purpose in life

Not knowing their only purpose was to build a planet technologically advanced such as their mother planet

And when these inhabitants would finally become as advanced as their superiors

Their ancestors would come and begin killing Planet Z with their oil-drilled dreams

*What if we are living on Planet Z?*

# Tendencies

Sometimes
Sometimes I wish my soul could take a swim
in the fountain of youth because my past life
has been such a burden
Sometimes
Sometimes my spirits are seemingly
searching for sanity by studying Sufi poets
And I'm reaching for ridiculous reasons to
relate to these Rumi poems
And you
You might not know how it feels to be tested
on a daily basis
Because as a man society is quick to watch us
fall
But slow to see us rise
Many have fallen to the gardens of greed
Lands of lust
Empires of envy
But not I
Not I Not I Not I
For I use my open eye to open eyes
Eyes like the full moon when my friends were
staring at medusa
Stoned to the thought of the future
It's depressing
It's depressing to take an anti-depressant

knowing you're not effective as a human
being
My white blood cells are molding into the
multiple medications prescribed by my
physician
And in my position I lack attention
When I should be at ease but all I need is
someone to about face to ask what's wrong
Karma works in wonderful ways
Never the hit it and quit it kind of guy
because I can't handle the tears running
down my daughters eyes
I turn down offers to turn up every weekend
I could be drinking a lot of liquor
I could me smoking a lot of weed
My life could be more exciting but
I don't want my son to end up like me
And I start to wonder
Maybe everyone has been in my position
Thinking about lives with your absence
Not suicidal thoughts
But a life that's lifeless
Despite the numerous killings by life's every
aspect
I'm hanging on every tear I drop
Suffocating on every sorrow I got
I just want to sit in my garage and let the
smoke get me high
Pressing my life on the pedal till death gives

me a ride
Or jump off a roof and think about you as I'm
falling to my fate
Or maybe even
Or maybe even sit in my tub and take a bath
with my music on blast
And just drop the radio so the sound of
electricity can spark my veins
I'm not dark and insane I'm human
And it's humane to contemplate a life that's
given
So taking my own isn't theft when out is the
only thing left
And before death you're left with your last
words
The mic is a weapon and I hold it towards my
enemy
And I ask myself
If what I'm doing right here
Right now
Is my purpose in life

# Late For Class

He would wake up every morning and have the same box of cereal

He would pack up his bag that consisted of a book full of poems that made his uncertain future acceptable

He missed his bus that day

Worried he wouldn't make it to his class full of undecided majors

He quickly jumped on the next bus full of 8 hours shifts and the scent of Starbucks

A woman running towards the bus screamed at the driver yelling him to stop, and he did

She walked in and grabbed the attention of every middle class man reading the paper

Her brown complexion and her grass root eyes sat right next to the student

He wanted to sit right next to her for as long as he can

Thinking of how to scheme up a sentence
without sounding stupid he missed his stop

After 30 minutes of thinking about the most
effective statement he suddenly said

Do you know what time it is?

She laughed because she didn't want to start
a conversation first

That day, he realized whose laugh he wanted
to hear for the next 40 years of his life

*Sometimes the wrong bus can take you the
right way*

# January 2013

My body peeled back the bed sheets like an
orange and found home in your sweetness

You told me you loved me that night

We talked for hours and even the silence in
our conversation turned into stories that
made us smile a bit longer than intended

# Sunrise

Just like the sun I have rose

Just like the sun I have rose from the East

And I will someday rest in the West

But with you I am the garden

And you are the sun

You encourage the growth of my stems

Does it bother you that we haven't met yet

# I Hate Love Poems

Within my dreams I had the sight to find the cite where we would recite our poetic vows

The same place where I'll walk you down the aisle and spend our honeymoon in an exotic isle

A place where the weightless waves wash up our arks onto the seductive sands

And the mountains around me shape the arc on your body

Just give me a peek, so I can help you reach your peak, and overtime pick up the pieces that provided you peace

A man is weak if he decides to waste his time, to place his hands below your waist, rather than spending weeks to find what's really inside

Lightening the pressure to find what sparks your mind and how I can create lightning to your enlightening pressure

*Don't love the idea of someone*

# The Brightness In My Roots

My ancestors have raised me to understand
that my skin resembles the earth that life
rises from

And my roots should not be like stars that
shine only in the moment of darkness

# When I Look In The Mirror

I've read that our minds make us 5x more
attractive when we look in the mirror.
So who am I?
Am I happy with whom I've become?
Do I have the same dreams as I did when I
was younger? Would my 6th grade self be
satisfied with the man that I am? The lights
above only layer my insecurities until the
lights turn off.
From that moment all I see is my shadow
conversing with my spirits about my deepest
secrets.
My mirror feeds me egotistical plates as I
sink in my own fear. Mirror...
**M**y
    **I**nsecurities
       **R**idiculously
         **R**iding
           **O**n
             **R**eality
You can stylize your insecurities with
materialism. But know this, satisfy yourself
before you satisfy your enemies. Reflect
yourself in order to help yourself. Don't let
the mirror bring you down, let it help you
pick up the pieces that define you. Let all

your worries down the drain and set your confidence on the counter. Pick it up every morning and let it rest every night. Look at yourself every day, I mean really look at yourself. Know that today you are better than you've ever been. Don't let the darkest spaces in your mind defeat you and don't let the lightest parts of your heart lower you.

# Saudade

I have read

I have read that the inability to accept loss is
a form of insanity

So I must be crazy if my schedule consists of
working from 6am to 3pm

Attempting to find a balance from 3pm to
6pm

Eating food that's slowly killing me at 7pm

Reading books to erase the stories from your
fingerprints the moment you were touched
by my poems from 8pm to 10pm

Write powerful poetry from 10pm to 2am

And have empty dreams from 2am to 4 am

Hoping

Just hoping my mind doesn't find the time to
think about you

# The Feeling Of Sleeping Next To Damaged

Girl, when I wake up next to you the first

thing I notice is

How your breath smells like shit!

And how the hair on my legs is rubbing

against yours and I wake up everyday a bit

more frustrated

If only I can look at you the way I look at you

when we're not home

Social gatherings lead to multiple hours

above the sink where your

shallowness sinks deeper than my

insecurities

Walking with confidence when you're by my

side because all my boys come up to me like

"Damn Sal, is that you?!"

"Is that who you're fucking with?"

If only they knew that the devil in a new

dress is just a gold digger

with an invisible tiara fascinated by my

family jewels

Don't find it unusual that she barely walks

past the bathroom as if the mirror taunts her

ego

and judges her personality rather than the

heavy bags that she carries

Heavy bags above her reconstructed nose

symbolizes abusive relationships

A sore throat that isn't from one-night stands

But every night when she can barely stand

forcing fingers down her mouth

*I learned that she was broken, but who am I
to fix her?*

# Acceptance

My soul has found
comfort in knowing my
vehicle has done so much good
and committed even more destruction

# Redefine

I am appalled by the modern day reaction to poetry

I have written poems to prove that watered down thoughts are more refreshing than a drop of purity hanging from a poets tree

These poems aren't suitable for adolescent minds that can't tie abstract ideas below their collar

Which is why my poems are frustrated

Sentences that provide food for thought can't be held by a short attention span

And

Your doctoral degree is pointless the moment my tongue formulates sentences that questions your scientific theory

Remember this poem the next time you read a group of words on tumblr or when you watch a youtube video that lacks substance and think that it is true poetry

# Neighborhood Watch

one of the longest trends that this nation has
been wearing

will not be displayed on twitter

or drowned in a bucket of ice water above
your head

home will become less hashtags and more toe
tags

when crooked cops are in your hood killing all
of your friends

# Facing The Devil

I'm afraid to go outside and become another statistic

Where my brown skin is a target for misguided individuals who use fear as their motive

As if our relationships are run by politicians who have a drive to take these "United States" into an un-united state and use unity as an excuse to utilize foreign land

I represent broken dreams built on rich schemes that have put my brothers and sisters out of a place to eat

I'm afraid of force-fed lies as ghosts of Guantanamo grapple the government

I step outside and I see more gang signs than street signs

Although my future is a reoccurring Rubik's cube taunted by the twister of destiny I'm trying to monopolize my life until I get that call

*If a dance with the devil might last forever,
I'll take a trip down hell's gates and live on
that level*

# Letter To My Son

I look up to the sun in hopes to see you in the future. You've been such a huge part of my life without actually being in my presence and I hope for one thing; that you don't ever end up like your father. Don't let this country that is currently controlled by currency cloud your character. You are a king just like your ancestors. You are a creator amongst yourself and those around you. I walk everyday as if your shadow stands behind me every second of my life. It would take 9 months for you to arrive, and you'll be the 1 upon my arrival. 9+1 does not equal 10. It equals 1 with a circle next to it. 1 represents knowledge. Because knowledge is always recycled and you are also a reflection of my wisdom, mistakes, achievements, regrets, and everything else until you enter my life. Don't do what I've been doing...

*Don't be the reason why your mother cries in her room so often*

# February 2013

We have not been talking as much

You say there is something in the air

But I don't feel a thing

Why do you taste the toxins
in a room full of clarity

# Revolution Starts With You

I sit in class every day hoping not to
regurgitate some "rich" shit from professors
who can't teach for shit

I'm not fit for four walls and multiple-choice
tests that determine who I am

Go to school or go to prison are the words
instilled within my neighborhood

But what's the difference when you're taught
to be caught

Women tend to place me in their past because
my future is uncertain

Never will I apologize for working with the
youth because

You can change the president and you can
change the mayor

But actual **change** comes from the bottom up

Change your community to change your
country

*Fuck being 41, waking up, just to smother some bosses*

*You can catch me making change outside your governor's office*

# Her Side Of The Bed

Love
 Is like
  A dream
   You wake up
    Remembering the
     Smallest details on a
     Random Tuesday
     Morning
    And a man
   Can be in-between
  A woman's legs and
 Still can't understand where
She's coming from

# If Only You Knew

It seems as if these words that provide a plate
of understanding comes off my tongue so
easily for those who read my poems

As if my words were more of a gift than a
curse

As if my words can't massage out your
thoughts and rub you wrong at the same time

As if I don't have pages of poems that expose
the conversations I have with the devil that
keeps reminding me how much we're alike

As if I wish for women to love the idea of me
rather than me

As if these words were more for you than
they are for me

*Poetry holds so much power for a poor-*
*peoples art form*

# Without me

I tried writing you an apology letter once
It is now stuck in between everything else I'm
too ashamed to remember
And though the rotten fruit that has become
a burden might not reach your garden
Know that you will remain replenished
without it

# She Loved Me For My Jewelry

If a man is knowledge

A woman must be wisdom

Together we give birth to understanding

In hopes to raise freedom

Justice must be served plates of

Equality that maintain

Food for thought and

Clothing that consists of righteousness

With shelter built from bricks carved by
angels to

Harness love that demons attempt to
plagiarize

The reproduction of peace

Supports life long conversations of happiness

*Today there is no chance for games when my tongue twisters recite*
*a body of hymns that moves her like a morning ritual*

# Occasional Asshole

I'll be honest

Sometimes I want to fuck these easy hoes but
even that's a hard decision

But I cant be the dude who decides to sleep
with indecisive women

Because their decisions are far from a mother

And though I'm a hopeless romantic, I believe
that true love is absent

So I practice abstinence, in hopes that one
girl will notice I prefer happiness

Before I put her hair in a mess

I can't handle this stress

See as I'm pursuing higher education, they
say that's the time to get high and start
penetrating but that's not me

My heart pumps my past mistakes

My lungs are full with all the shit that I used
to take so

Every time I take the time to give a woman a
chance

I start to suffocate so forgive me

Forgive me if I let distance become an issue
or if your ass isn't as fat as I want it to

Or if I look for things wrong with you

Forgive me

Because my perfect woman is based on the
acceptance of those around me

So maybe I'm the problem

Or maybe it's the type of women I started to
meet cuz

I've met those who love when you play with
their hair like the strings of a violin

But they're too addicted to the income of drug
dealing men or

Those who only look good in photographs, but when you look at them eye to eye

There's nothing to focus on behind the lenses

I've even met girls who cover up their past with excessive makeup

But don't have enough space for a foundation

From singers who satisfy the sentimental chapters of my secluded soul but cant seem to find the same page

To painters who promote writing poems with brushes rather than pens

Brushing the base that balances dreams and reality, but somehow cant draw and design a future close to home

It seems like every woman I've met have been dealt too many cards

Chased by too many jokers, settled for a jack, and folded on one of a kind

The kind who would do more than strip you of
your thoughts to put their hands on your
learning curve

I'm numbing the nerves that have the nerve
to foreshadow the past

History seems to repeat itself

Meeting the person of your dreams too early
in your life

The time isn't right or the distance makes it
worse

Ruining every chance I have with someone
who could've been my wife

Shit

I'm feeling like I didn't send that chain letter
text message back in middle school and now
I'm cursed for the next 20 years of my life

Honestly... does it make me less of a man that
I believe the wrong road to a woman's heart
is a trip down her pants?

For I cant take that chance

They say you are what you eat

But the guys who get the most pussy are the biggest dogs that I know

Summarizing my uncharted notebook that leaks tears of past relationships and holds blanks pages that represent what could've been

I've lost peace with all those who meant something to me

You might not know how it feels to be cheated out of your destiny

But it explains why I continue to have asshole tendencies

I'm still someone who's hopelessly holding on to find something within

In hopes to define and describe what love is when the nice guy wins

# Our Last Fight

She's begging me to move on but what the fuck am I supposed to do with 370 pages of poems

208 hours, 35 minutes, and 56 seconds of conversation I had with you

She's begging me to move on but I just don't know how and today people have the audacity to ask me

Sal, why don't you have a girlfriend?

Usually my poems are just stories but to be honest I can't keep this bottled in

Because she left me February 14th, 2010

At 2 am

Because of a drunk driver on the corner of Florin and Power Inn

*The story you don't want to remember, but can't seem to forget*

# Daily Basis

Is it just me or
We spend half of our time finding our other
half to spend half of our lives with,
at half the right age
I catch myself writing more "love poems"
when I have nobody to love
What am I supposed to do when my peers are
pursuing people who will never love them
back?
What am I supposed to do when you're with
someone who's sharing his or her energy with
others?
What am I supposed to do?
I can see myself sharing a cup of tea with you
just like my grandparents do.
But I won't give you the time of day.
I beg of women not to fall in love with me
because honestly,
I've broken too many hearts into pieces that
couldn't be picked up by the person they
belong to.
As hard as it seems, I don't do this on
purpose.
I'm just broken as the rest of you.

*Why is it so hard to admit that we're battling our demons on a daily basis?*

# Not Too Long Ago

i promised you

i wouldn't write any

poems about you

but I lied and wrote a book instead

# Public Announcement

I have millions of poems but most of you folks
look for the "ooh's" and "ahh's" and ask if my
words are true or not
Everyday I swallow my pride and try to
paraphrase my life into a couple of poems
I get nervous before I get on stage but at one
point that wasn't a problem
Strangers know more about me than my
friends do
Poor in paper but my words are rich like the
land along the Nile when the river was
flooded
Too many of you guys find home in my pieces
of work and
I'm forever in debt for the love you show
The same love that I find hard to reciprocate
Sometimes I wish I can cut off my tongue and
never let my lips leave you with hope
These poems I write are from the moments
like
When I asked her if she loved me and her
silence spoke sentences that the English
language couldn't comprehend

*Those eyes that spoke of freedom are now covered by the prison bars you call eyelashes*

# 84

How many women do you know that live in widows colony?

How about children living in the streets because that's where home used to be?

Waiting for mom and dad to come home in time...

But their parents shared so many bullets they couldn't be identified.

Streets screamed,

Why'd you take my mother?

Why'd you take my daughter?

Why'd you take my son?

Why'd you take my father?

The sun as red as the devil

It rained the ashes of burnt flesh and holy scriptures upon the gravel today

*You don't know how it feels to be known as the only silent letters of this world's vocabulary*

# My Love, Forgive Me

Oh how ironic this world is
For the universe has gifted me with words
that explain the space
in between the stars and the humanity under
your fingernails
All these beautiful words, but I couldn't find
any
when I needed them the most


Everything I wish not to be, I have become

# Angels in the City

The beggar
who sticks his hands
in a pile of trash
to find bread
for the feathers that fly
before he stuffs his beak
is the richest man I know

# Confusion

Let confusion
Speak to you like
A morning prayer that
You recite every morning

# My Schedule

My daily schedule is very simple

Brush my teeth and take mouthwash to rid
my ancestors' addiction to alcohol

Eat a plate of pencils to produce poems for
you people on the daily

Drop my habits and throw on the twelve
jewels of Islam

Fill my car with anything that will take my
mind off of you

Sit in a classroom full of debt and hope to
obtain a degree that will provide my life with
some depth

Stand on stage and show why a poet is so
good with his tongue

Take a shower and wash off every regret I've
ever had to face

Read a book to sharpen the tools that have
failed to erase your fingerprints

Post a poem in hopes for one person to not just read and comment but to ask me something preferably anything

*Don't let this preoccupied lifestyle make you forget how to be human*

# March 2013

A few friends told me that we should have
talked a bit more

That

We would still be together
if we took a few step backs to realize

We took the wrong exit too early

And the road we have been driving on
was full of stone placed by everyone but us

# The Biggest Illusion

People often tell me I am great at creating
stories
That the sentences stretch far past periods
like wartime art
that speaks home for veterans who never
adjusted back
to a home cooked meal
Maybe there is magic in-between the lines
The paper as a well lit stage and the
writer as the magician
Watch me split characters in half just to show
the world the
creatures living in their organs
The magician is the illusion
He will grab the simplest words and pull
rabbits out of the rhetoric
And release a dozen doves after each literary
device


*The illusion does not exist in the words it
lives in the children who find magic without
them*

# Misguided

I apologize
For all of my brothers around the world
Who have fallen to misdirection
And found solace in the pants of a queen

I have introduced myself to women
That have hands in the shape of fear

They hesitate the moment I
Wrap my celibate arms around their
Apprehensive body


*My brothers don't know that temples have
been carved from spirits of their mothers*

# Stars And Stripes They Said

The photos have faded since the last time I let
them breathe
Scrapbooks on top of scrapbooks
They fade every time I want to visit old
friends
I once gave my childhood friend a call and he
answered to my surprise
I asked him to tell me anything
He continued to tell me that he regrets
leaving home
His friends have been conditioned to accept
human bones that wash up
on the shore of the countries they visit
every morning he would make his rounds
My childhood friend became an eagle in the
sky
And this is all he ever wanted
Family members back home would jump like
he used to when they heard another soldier
losing his life in battle
He would enter foreign countries the way the
pledge of allegiance would enter the
mouths of children every morning

# SEXUAL LANGUAGE

DAMN
And I mean DAMN
The things I would do to her
I mean the things I would do to her
I would tear her insecurities and suck on her
personality
I would even kiss her thoughts for hours
and just hope it leads to the bedroom
where the headboard bounces off the wisdom
walls
as we scream our own philosophical beliefs
Giving her mind a massage
I'll provide an intellectual relief
And to be honest
I love how great she is at oral
As in she knows how to keep a conversation
As in she turns me on with her dialect
Because she knows
That I know how to use my dic-
tionary
With her vo-
cabulary
The way I run my fingers through her pages
I'll lick her letter till she gets the message
I want to undress her brain and go down on
her thoughts

just so my poets tongue can get a taste of
reality
I'll let her feelings get on top and ride my
emotions
and keep switching positions until we reach
our climax
Knowing my ass in less than five minutes
The things I would do to her in bed
most dudes cant do
I want to penetrate her inner, and deeper
dreams
and help them become true
And I want to pull her hair as if love
Love is at the tip of her scalp
See there's no need to wear a hat
because I know where my heads at
Engaged with her brain beyond any measure
She's a virgin and this is how I give her
pleasure

# Don't Humanize God

I had a conversation with God the other day

I was reminded that Heaven has its own distinct sound

Voices that don't share sounds of males and females but

A language that is spoken between land and water

I was told that we fall on springs when there are some more reasons to rise on our own

I was told that we've been looking at life with the wrong set of eyes

Water is actually colored by complexions of different communities

Clouds are evaporated prayers

Wind is the warmth of angels walking with their wings tucked under our skin

*Humans are scriptures who sacrifice stars to summon the sanity of each other's souls*

# Letter To My Unborn Daughter

A father is supposed to tell his daughter to
stay away from men who have the ability to
formulate words in a way that makes this
world a little smaller and the soul a little
more discernible.
But I hope a woman that looks like
satisfaction for a complex man with simple
needs and smells like why I shouldn't regret
making time for women would take a chance
with a man who eats indecisiveness for
dinner in hopes that one day
I can give you this letter.
I just want you to know that your wrists have
been shaped by the same spirits of Gods and
your heart has been held together by every
little thing your father tried to do right.
I hope you can learn from your mistakes to
walk down a road carved by knowledge and
molded by the spirits of natives who harness
the sun.


*If he treats you like a queen, never be more
than friends. If he truly understands your
roots, he'd treat you like a soldier instead*

# #Follow

I'm exhausted and disappointed
that the world won't explore outside the
window to focus on the galaxy because
everyone wants his or her hands on the next
iPhone
Too many birds sitting on vines to tweet the
latest trends
Too many assholes attempting to ruin your
day, anonymously of course
Too many direct messages to grab attention
rather than messages with direct intentions
And the only stories you know of are 6
seconds long
Feeling connected only when my Wi-Fi has a
strong connection
The world has forgotten that strangers fall to
double taps over grams every day
Apps can't filter the bullshit in your
personality
Status is measured by the amount of likes,
rather than your accomplishments
We memorize passwords more than past
words.
Minimizing people like letters that we fit in a
box that can only hold 140 characters
I want to hear your voice, rather than read

what you have to say
Our conversations are based on irrelevance
we have made relevant
I never thought my space would become
insignificant.


*Is it difficult for you to wake up without your
phone every morning?*

# Anniversary

I sometimes ask myself how my mornings would be by your side, but then I remember the nights my pulse would indulge in the tone of your voice and how I wake up the following day without you just fine

# Bystander

My friend only heard laughter when the
school bell would ring

He would walk to class with a handful of
confidence to handle cruelty

My friend would take notes just to erase the
fingers that were pointed at him

Jokes turned into threats

And threats turned into depressing threads
that were sewed into his spine

The internet made him feel like he was in
their net every time they distracted their
own insecurities

Every day I watched him walk home with his
head lower than the morals of his bullies

Every day he would beat around the bush
when his parents asked about his bruised
pupils

Every day he would write poems, but never

found the vocabulary to explain his anxiety

Every day I wish I took the time to be his
friend

*The only time I see him is when I lay a garden
of regret next to his gravestone*

# The Usual Bollywood Movie

Glowing melanin about 9:55 in the morning
as I overheard you talking about skipping
class
I never told you but I ran into you on purpose
just so you can spill your hot coffee on my
new red sweater
Hoping
Just hoping
You can laugh it off and
we would connect off simple theories on life
outside the university
coffee shop
And we did
But now I wish I never craved coffee that
morning
Do you remember our neighbors
Every night they wished we didn't have a
home full of violence
Now every night they listen to a home full of
silence
And I swear if I can hold on to you like I hold
On to my words
I would
But some things are better left unsaid
And this love, which is in your nature to ruin
needed to end

*The sun shines bright just to remind you of your shadow*

# The Black Box

The black box in the room that has killed the
culture of a family dinner has been lying to
you

It creates beautiful images that will occupy
life between walls to restrain the sound of
harmony in the streets

Monsters live behind that box to instill fear in
the lungs of birds that were once populated
with revolutionary rites

Do not point to guns when the triggers have
been pulled by the system that have failed to
foster our feathers

# April 2013

Today is my birthday

And you did not have much to say

How selfless I thought you were

# Voice For The Voiceless

A day that changed my life forever
A day where I was too young to comprehend
what I visualized on the television set
An attack on the twin towers that somehow
held the balance of not just this country
But the fate of innocent civilians all around
the world
Buildings that were side by side
Half and half
And the aftermath was all that we had in the
end
Planes that were piloted by prejudice, hatred,
and injustice
Flew into these same towers that created a
dark and thick smoke in the sky
So when I prayed for peace there wasn't a
reply
And as soon as these towers dropped along
with my handles
Accusations were made of every Indian and
Middle Eastern Individual as a radical
I'm not just talking about the brown people
I'm giving a voice to the voiceless
My people the Sikh people
That never desired evil and emphasized the
equal

So why are we the target of these crosshairs
Is it because people are scared of another
attack
When we have no apparent relevance to these
attacks
How can you violate one who wears a turban
which he/she wraps every morning with
honor and sustains it with his/her pride
How can you violate one who grows his/her
beard that symbolizes a gift from God
How can you
Violate one who might holster a dagger,
which isn't used as a weapon but serves the
same purpose as a peace sign
Or a closed fist in the air
A stand for the truth
And slowly this land of opportunity has
molded itself into a place where you will
always feel like a visitor
Because even if you were born here you
might still live the life of an immigrant
But to whom
This nation is controlled by the same gang
that promotes a democracy
Upholds an hypocrisy
Advertises prosper and change
But leaves our pockets empty handed
So how can you accuse people of what they
are not

How can you kill your own when in fact we're
all brothers and sisters
Act on what is given
Represent what my ancestors have read and
written
It is that all men are the same
It is through error they appear different
All men have the same eyes
The same ear
The same nose
A compound built from wind
Water
Fire and earth
It's the one god who created it all
Let no man
Even by mistake
Suppose there is a difference

# Our Last Fight Part Two

Inbox full, missed calls, my perspective of
something gone wrong
Haven't seen her in months and haven't
talked in so long
Before she left on her trip we fell into an
altercation
Hiding something so we pushed each other
around
And she left my arms with lacerations
A week has slipped by and her family came
back home
Promised myself tomorrow I would show my
apologized eyes
So when I did
When I stepped into the house I can feel the
sorrow
I can hear the silence that still suppresses the
beat of my heart
Looked around in confusion, asked questions
because I was worried
And started yelling in fear
They said sit down son there's something you
need to hear
There's been an accident
A drunk driver hit her on the driver's side
the car flipped a couple times and she didn't

survive
My heart dropped as soon as my soul did but
it got worse
They said someone else died
I ask was it a father, brother, mother, sister,
or wife
They told me my unborn child also lost its life
I cried to the state of no emotion and it killed
me more than anything else
She was afraid to tell me in fear that I would
leave them like how her father left her
Months passed by and I've lost myself
She didn't just leave with a part of me


She left me without the chance of being a
great father to our family

# Displaced

My heart is displaced

I've found myself juggling different women in different locations

Till I find the one that's different with a little bit of patience

She said she's impatient, but she'll wait for me

But this whole concept of time is the reason for my displaced heart

Waiting till the time is right has led to unfinished business

And now here I am

Within hours away from someone who is living a lifetime away

Telling me she'll wait

But with wait comes the possibility of men who aren't me

And the possibility of women who aren't you

If not soon, then in another lifetime

*But how many times have we said that in our
past lives*

# 360 Senses

I would have never imagined the grief my
skin has experienced, as well as the ecstasy
my lungs have had the pleasure to meet in
the same year. We've lost touch with hands
that have once felt like home and adopted
species that fly within our bones just
so we know how to feel again. I know of
mirrors that watch children with more
caution than parents do. My knees have
introduced themselves to more funerals than
moments of prayer. The language I speak
cannot comprehend the poetry in the silence
of a grieving widow. The pupils above my
nose cannot visualize the poetry in the wave
of an ocean. But the words in this world have
provided revolutions in the minds of young
men and woman continuing to face adversity
the moment the sun opens their eyes.

*I've been too busy finding the poetry in
everything around me*

# I Wrote This Instead

We don't talk as much anymore and I've accepted that. Sometimes I stare at my phone in hopes to find an excuse to start a conversation. Maybe you might be doing the same thing right now.

# Forgotten Letter

Around 7:46 every day my hands begin to tremble. I can't remember when they started to become weaker, but these poems became constellations I began to connect. The signs took me to a space where dark matter imitated the lines on my palms that were once read by beings that understood the light. I am not sure if my hands cringe because they need to write or if they are too exhausted by digging deep into my skin.

*My hands have become aftershocks since the last time we met*

# The Difference

You spoke sentences the moment you smiled

that my Sufi-like symbolism couldn't sustain

Usually I'm great at formulating thoughts

but I couldn't wrap my finger around the idea
of you

All you wanted was the three words I thought
I'd never say

Eight letters that loved to lay at the tip of my
tongue as if they were meant to caress you
every moment you doubted yourself

Men and women are genetically split by 3%

This 3 % is the rib of Adam

This 3% is the dot in the yin-yang symbol

This 3% is such a tiny amount yet the only
reason why men don't understand women

How can I explain that God has given me an

exam I've been studying for throughout my
life

But when I opened the first page of you

I was asked questions that were beyond my
comprehension

*Why hide the pain when you can appreciate
the scars*

# May 2013

I have kissed someone who does not remind
me of you

We are happy

She is everything you wanted to become

Her lips consist of qawwalis

And her love reflects a story only Waris Shah
would create

# She Is Scarred

It's Monday
This is a story about a girl who happens to be
the happiest girl on campus
But she came to class late exactly at 9:45
Because her dad threatened her 9 times with
the .45
So all she wore was tears created by fear
And a mouth full of blood that was woven by
pain
Seeing her cry forever scarred my life

It's Tuesday
Her name is Jasmine
And Jasmine happens to be a has been
Who has been happy before but now she's
suffering
Because her mother is struggling
And her father is violent in his own home
She's too afraid to call 911 so she disregards
the phone
And when he beats her
She takes hits of her own just to relieve the
stress

It's Wednesday
Everyone knows the reason why she's always

102

late
Because her silence screams the saddest
story
I've heard till this day
Screams that are louder than any school bell
ringing
Quietest amongst hundreds of kids
But her footsteps seems to be the loudest it's
sickening

It's Thursday and have I seen her
Honestly it's been awhile
She's been there trying to cover up new
things
But the deepest scar she's been trying to hide
is her smile and she's so oblivious
She's oblivious to the fact that she's easy to
understand but hard to find
And as her grades dropped
Her marks increased
And all you can see is that her clothing
consisted of nothing but long sleeve
Which made things just a little more obvious

It's Friday and on top of this
It hurts me more when he hits her
Because Jasmine isn't just some random girl
at school
So when child services busted through the

door
They told me I couldn't see my sister
anymore

It's Saturday
She's back home with a mindset of her own
Her life is consisted of nightmares
And her dreams are created by fables
Because all she thinks of is that someday
Some guy will look at her as an angel
And put an halo around her finger
Up all night making rounds around the house
And all I tell myself is,
Let her be, let her be, let her be
For I can't come in-between what I believe
isn't apart of me

It's Sunday
Her birthday
I pray to God each and every day
But for some reason God wasn't beside me
I woke up to my mother's silence
The stench of something different
And as I run downstairs to find out what's
wrong
I see a new decoration hanging above my
living room wall
My sister
And it kills me because I could've stopped all

of this
Everyone knew how she felt
But I didn't
Because I am
I am
I am
Too selfish to realize what a real brother is

# Irony

I have been born in a country that taught me
how to forget my native tongue
The culture of our people is a joke when worn
on the skin that resembles soil
But "exotic" and "beautiful" when displayed
on privileged bodies

# Monday

My eyes have introduced themselves to only
ten hours of sleep these last few days. Cups of
coffee have been conversing with my lips
more than usual. Walking with friends have
become moments to complain about school
and love while reflecting on why our sheets
move around more often. The harder I work,
the lazier my skin becomes.
It is 7am
I am awake
Today is only Monday
Today is fucking Monday

# We Are Wrong About Love

They didn't tell you that the breakup itself is
the easiest part

Mornings waiting for messages that were
tailored for the shape of your skin

Nights replaying voicemails from missed calls
that you miss the most

Listening to music that reminds your organs
that you will not love the same way

Telling yourself that everything will be back
to normal when you know it is a lie

*Is the hardest part*

# June 2013

A few months have gone by and I'm doing well

I hope you are too

You have been keeping in touch more often

I don't know how to tell you that I have found love in someone else

So I stopped keeping in touch

# Solidarity

In some countries where women

Drown in deep oppression

Daughters seem to understand

The waters of a patriarchal ocean

While sons continue to swim in it


Teach your brothers how to fight next to the
women who have raised them

# This Is How He Described Her

She wore the sound of wind around the shape
of her waist
Flames would scar the streets her feet would
press upon
The smell of earth would rise from her
presence
Water grew from her head and my god the
depth that flowed past her shoulders was full
of sunken ships and
Treasures that men would sacrifice their
hands for

# The Writers Side

Dreams are difficult to forget

but nightmares are easy to remember

Sorrow will leave the soul sleepless

like villages that scream struggles

in the form of poetry

And the memories that kept us awake

will slowly become short lines in a journal

that was forgotten the moment one found a

new reason to write

# Temporary Farewells

Are you content
Are you content with sleepless nights that
consist of
"What if's"
And unanswered questions that flood your
mind

The longer you attempt to keep your head
above the water
The harder it becomes to stay alive
So face the unknown clouding your feet
And the darkness following you every day

Lose yourself in the depth of the unknown
But know that someday
You might come back like waves reaching for
the sand
To discover the fossils we once called
footprints

# English Class Blues

There is an island inside of my English professor, an island full of different species that have found home in her organs. There are animals that swing on her veins and swim in her thoughts. There are trees that grow out of her skin. I tell her that the trees are gifts from the universe. Her broken bones have become fertilizer for flowers. In this island, there are no fossils, no animals that have become extinct, and there are no visitors. This island floating behind her chest gave life to her lungs. I will never know when she discovered this island, but I will always remember the day she had to leave.

# July 2013

We were supposed to discuss a few things

But I became busier than I usually do

And you had your eyes set on a future that didn't include me

So we never spoke about it

# The Depth

All that one learned to grasp
Drowned to the deepest and darkest parts of
the ocean
Whatever was left surfaced to kiss the
uncontrollable body of water

And one day
Someone will lose themselves within the
darkest parts of the ocean
Just to find what one left many years ago
And a lifetime of research will never discover
its purpose

*I think this is what I've been floating on for so
long*

# Photosynthesis

A Flower
must understand
its roots to grow
so I channel who I am
and who I once was, and
learned that to become
a great man
begins with
becoming a better son

# Lost in Lahore

I'm reminded of it every morning
In the face of a child who plays tag with his
shadows

And between the lips of long lost lovers

I visualize it in the heart of men who
transition too soon

I hear it in the lies of those who run your
country

I can't understand why love and death feel
like comfort

My skin mourns for what was
and celebrates what might be


*The amount of details in my pieces might be
reflections from a past life*

# Roll Call

Dear Professor,

My father and mother raised their child

With empty pockets and dreams of a degree

So I will not apologize if my colored skin has

To correct you on the first day of school

Before you identify me as,

"Excuse me if I mispronounce your name"

I couldn't receive voicemails because my
inbox was full

So at 4am I decided to replay all the messages
that proved to me once again the love we had
was genuine

And then I deleted them all

# The Smell of Flowers

Funerals. Funerals. Funerals.

Candlelight vigils and marches for those

Who have found home underneath flowers

Flowers that sleep above boxes buried six feet

Deep

Now I am stuck with

Shattered dreams

Fixed promises

And a shitload of answered questions


The first time I bought her flowers was also
the last

# My Soul Resides in Egypt

My soul left my body the other night and
swam to the side of the world where
a civilization found the answer

After walking through the hall of history that
sits under the right paw

The archives of Atlantis branded the wrists of
my soul

My soul came back to me the minute before I
woke up and drowned in 60 seconds of
dreams

These dreams told me that there was once a
civilization that told us that there is two of
everything

Pillars that were in pairs of twos and
pyramids that was home to this world and
another

And the Sphinx that faces the rise of the sun
has been living life without ever knowing
his partner that faces the fall of the sun
has not been discovered yet

# In Too Deep

Do not come

Swimming back to me

When he leaves you wet like an ocean

Hoping he hands you the world

When it is the moon

That makes your water rise

# Maybe

**Maybe** I will never know what you did with
my letters
Or the photos of me you once had on the wall
**above** your bed
Maybe I will never know how it feels to run
my fingers
Through your hair after **a** random Sunday
morning anymore
Maybe I will never know if you shared your
lips
with a **man** who does not understand
Your disinterest in, wait I will let him figure it
out
Maybe I will never know how it feels to **love**
again
Maybe you **will**
Maybe I am the only one who **write**s a poem
full of maybes
Maybe all **you** will ever be is an idea
Maybe I will meet you in **another** life to give
life to what this once was
**Maybe**, just maybe you are feeling the same
way as I at 11:58pm

# Future Reminders

Some of those who are meant to serve and
protect
Might be the same one's aiming for your neck

Chains were never erased
Just changed to the color of gold

And how life is like love
It enters least expected
And leaves the same way

A few things to remind my children

# My Body is My First Home

My body is my first home
The only siblings I have are the thoughts in
my head
And the emotions pumping from my heart
My lungs up to my teeth imitate the scent of a
garden in the backyard I used to live in when
the front yard was a suicide mission
The blood running through my veins are like
all the reasons I argue with myself
My fingers aren't really mine they are yours
I've been touched by the presence of oxygen
shared in a room full of strangers
If my body is my first home, I must find gold
beneath the dirt


My body is my first home, but sometimes I
want to move away

# September 2013

The first day of school was set on a
Wednesday

And within the first week I saw you so many
times

The woman next to me in the library had the
same nose as you

The girl in my women studies class had the
type of attitude you would sometimes have

The beautiful stranger I had lunch with had
your smile

I couldn't stop staring at the woman in the
library

I made the girl in my class furious as much as
possible

I made the beautiful stranger laugh as much
as possible

Just so I can see you the way I did before we
went wrong

# The Dance My Hands Do

My hands
Choreograph themselves
To write poems so the rest of
My body can forget how
*"Numb"* feels

# Different Perspective

When I was a kid I used to create cities

Skyscrapers were recycled bottles

Bridges were stacks of books I never read

Roads were paved by limited edition Hot
Wheels racing tracks

Mountains were my dirty clothes

Each backyard had a

Swimming pool, a military base and a pet
dinosaur

People died for no valid reason

And the universe was my bedroom


Who said the human definition of the world is
the right one

# 16 Hours

The hair on the back of my neck sometimes
ponder how your hands will react to this book
if you ever have the courage to buy it
because you know many of these poems have
been inspired by your love as well as the
absence of it

# Look Closer

To write verses about

The texture of a poem

The scent of rain

The matras and sutras the clouds recite
before the sun says goodbye

Is ineffable in itself

# Where Have You Gone

The most
difficult time is
when one does not
have any of it
and how easy
it has become to waste what one has the most

# T R E E S

My brothers and sisters have trees growing
from their skin
Trees that branch out in different directions
are full of stories
Many of my brothers and sisters trim these
trees but let the roots grow beyond the earth
they come from
They are not thorns
They are flowers
My sisters aren't afraid to embrace the forest
on their arms and the garden on their faces
These beautiful plants aren't reflections of
the soil they grow from
But the creator who planted the seeds

# October 2013

Your friends asked me how I am doing

I told them that I am well

They said something about how you travelled
past mountains that resembled dimples

And found warmth in a land that was colder
than your usual bedroom

They tell me that they are worried

Because you found a man that is damaged
more than you'll ever be

And they want me to "talk" to you so you can
"come to your senses"

I refused to speak because in reality

He is all you ever wanted

# Don't Look Down

I want you to wake up tomorrow and
Approach the mirror like it is the top of a
mountain that
You have been climbing for as long as you
remember
And let the reflection of your eyes remind
you why
You wake up every morning
Let the shadows represent the apparitions of
your past lives
Stand tall and look at your regrets as if they
are
The rocks at the bottom of a mountain
And understand that today
You have conquered

# The Worst Feeling

There will be a moment in your life
Where you will be unable to feel
As if the part of you that expresses emotions
has suddenly vanished
You will not cry over things that would have
moved you in the past
You will feel empty even when your cup is
overflowing
You will not comprehend love when it is
inside of you
You will feel sorrow for the fragments that
have left your body


Numbness is the worst type of pain

# Sooner or Later

I have surrendered by your feet many
moments ago

Why do you conquer my siblings and diminish
the language that has been full of poetry

Why do you kidnap dreams of men and bring
them to your home

Why do you destroy the same home that you
stole

I hope you develop the technology to build a
mirror powerful enough to tell you

We are native to this earth and children of
the same sun

# Beauty vs Disaster

Plates shift to create dimples
on the face of this Earth
that will astound the wanderer

Earthquakes shake the foundations
beneath our feet
that form tsunamis in the eyes of those
affected


I am still trying to figure out which one you
are

# This Is Not About You

When my friends ask about you, I tell them
that you are doing well.
I remind them how easy it became to forget
you. Every time I mention to my friends how
insignificant you have become, they comfort
me. They comfort me because I am not a good
liar.
I tell them how it easy it became to forget the
poetry in our conversations.
I tell them how uncomplicated the process of
removing a touch feels like.
I tell them how painless it is to cut
discussions shorter than before.
I tell them how natural it is to remove love
from a human body.
I tell them how effortless it is to restrain from
calling you at 1 am.
I tell them how risking parts of myself in
hopes to build a life with you is child's play.
When my friends ask about you, I tell them
that you are doing well.
I remind them how it easy it became to forget
you

# November 2013 8:12pm

You didn't ask me how I was doing

Nor did you ask about my parents
like you usually do

As baffled as I am

Your lack of concern has been good to me

# The Verses

When my friends begin to share the sad
symphonies of breakups

I begin to share my own

We take turns and mention stories that
connect us

We assure each other that love will come
again

We laugh

Because these verses from songs that have
ended make us feel

Like our lives aren't as dark as they truly are

# The Cabin We Used To Visit

Cold nights were survived by the warm villages in the hearts of my friends. A cabin took our juvenile tongues every winter where the woods would escape in every moment of laughter, as we would gather around campfires in the backyards of our memories. These memories would spark flames in hopes that the heat would mold friendships into forever. We would spend our nights escaping in the conversation the moon would have with the stars and fall asleep when the sun kisses the land.

# Golden State

More black men are facing bars today than
were enslaved in 1850

Incarcerated for possessing the same thing
the government regulates

Failed public education leads to life in a
privatized system

Sell in your block and you will be stuck in a 6
by 8 cellblock

Working to create jeans, lingerie, and license
plates for $1.25 an hour

Profiting from people of color is this country's
biggest addiction

1 university

22 prisons


Welcome to the Golden State

# The Hidden Spot

Tonight there is mystery in the air
The stars are practicing yoga
The clouds have parted
The moon displays a different expression
Meteor showers have become the arrows of
cupids bow
They remind me of everything I used to wish
for
Just like every night
There is mystery in the air

Salvin Chahal

# Describing My Mother

My mother's love is rich like the soil in Egypt
when the Nile would flood

Her melanin resembles an early morning
sunrise

Hair that flows like the five rivers

Eyes that reflect abstract Rumi poetry

She is a healer on this Earth

I give thanks to my father

But my mother welcomed birth

# Breathing

Breathing is a language in itself

There is a moment where one takes their
breath for the first time

While another is taking their breath for the
last time

This language tells a story

Only the heart can provide words for

When the tongue does not comprehend

# The Continuing Season

We always prepare ourselves for the storm
We check the temperature the moment we
wake up
We put on some socks and begin to open the
closet
just to find the layers that make us feel alive
Our hair peeks out from the sweater to face
the mirror just to say good morning
The kitchen calls our name with warm cha
and a breakfast that makes you feel snowed
in
We always prepare ourselves for the storm
until we step outside

# How To Make A Better You

Open yourself

Move your stomach and liver aside

Find all the reasons you woke up this
morning

Wash off the regrets that have burned your
lips

Boil every moment you fell in love

In a pot molded by your hardened facade

Pour a cup of rich memories you have failed
to forget

Marinate the moments your eyes had the
pleasure to meet

And garnish your plate with prayers that

Have fed strength to the ingredients in your
feet

# After The Wind

Perhaps I will never know how you felt that morning, or which box of cereal you consumed before class. Did you let sadness escape your eyes? Or did depression hide behind your laughter? Maybe your favorite black dress wore your last sense of hope that afternoon. I wonder if a conversation you had with the poems I sent you gave you closure. Perhaps I will never know why you had your last meal with me that evening.


*The wind is missed after the movement it creates*

# The Flower Shop

I was there
My feet quickly found the wall covered in
assorted flavors of a fresh breath
My lips finally tasted the juice of the sweets
the last time I visited
As a kid I never thought I would be here again
Red sign and meat that found an ocean on ice
being tossed around while every tourist
watched
The aroma of this market made my hands
feel youthful again
I saw city dwellers in a building far from
home
It reminded me of Delhi
The hair on my neck stood up the moment I
ran into the places I thought we'd share the
sky in
I visited a few museums
I dragged my jetlag body to events I told
myself I wouldn't go to
I visited the place that had that note on the
chair
The woman at the flower shop recognized the
sound of my stomach
She told me that my insides didn't buzz as
much as they used to

She handed me purple and white tulips
hoping to find honey in a comb that once
existed
She looked confused
My fingers rejected the same flowers my
wings were once eager to carry
After listening to her eyes pity my heart for
forgetting the geometry of the comb
She handed me different stems
I was told that these special flowers might
help a woman who can't smell petals
She looked confused again
My fingers rejected the same flowers my
wings might have been eager to carry
She then continued to smile
She realized the bees inside me don't buzz as
loud as they did
And the flower I built my nest around
Produced nectar that isn't as sweet anymore

# December 2013

The lessons
I have learned
this year have come
from a lifetime of experiences

# Thank You

Every day I promised a poem for all of you to
read
I lied
My "poems" are just forms of a **P**oet **O**bscurely
**E**rasing **M**emories
Every day I struggled to remember why I
stab myself with stories just to
make sure those who emotionally kill
themselves are resurrected through my
words
Each and every day I contemplate my
creativity because
proofreading anxiety isn't something a
human is meant to do
Writing lines that depict the feeling of
balancing on heaven and hell
Being criticized for using words as blades to
surgically remove the sound of defeat
from my lungs
And now I'm giving you my book to read
A book that was written by pencils sharpened
from my deepest regrets
on pieces of paper that were cut from the
wildest jungles of revolutionaries and
united by every brother and sister violated
by a corrupt cop

Before I give you my book, know this
You might find scraps of yourself on every
page
You might find tears that have found its way
into sentences
You might find yourself in me


*Life is something you will never understand*
*But you are a poem*
*Write your destiny each and every day*

If you got this far, you probably read every page or decided to become a little curious. I gave you a piece of myself through my poems hoping the pieces would spark some sort of thought or emotion. I also decided to make each and every book unique and the only way that is possible is with your input. The next couple of pages are series of workshops. They range from detailed instructions to a simple unfinished sentence on the top of a random page. The reason I did this is because I encourage expression and I believe my workshops will help you discover parts of creative side. I will leave blank pages after every workshop for you to express how you're feeling, what you're afraid to say, or maybe something interesting that has happened recently. You don't have to follow my instructions if you don't want to. You wouldn't be reading this if it weren't for your support in the first place. I encourage you to write down anything you want whenever you want on these following pages. Help finish this book for me. Your words have meaning to me as if they are my own. Write your own dedication/introduction on page 5. If you would like to share, email your work to salvinchahal@gmail.com or anonymously at sal-c.tumblr.com

# Persona vs. Character

So I want you to ask yourself what is the difference between persona and character. Before you read what I have to say I want you to know that there are no wrong answers. You are the standard. You should treat these workshops as if they are free writes. Just keep writing until you cant write no more, and try not to think too much. I believe that persona is how you are viewed, or the image you try to create. Character is who you truly are an as individual. I will give you four sections, and I want you to write down as many words as you can under them. For example, under persona you would write down words that describe how you believe people basically view you. Under character you would write down words that describe who you truly are or what you would want people to know. Under fear and can't live without, I want you wrote write down anything that can be tangible or not.

Persona    Character    Fear    Can't live w/o

I want you to write a letter to someone you've never met before. It can be your future spouse/son/daughter/professor, god, etc. I want you to use the 8 words you selected and just write. Don't think too much just write. When you are finished using the 8 words just keep writing. This is an opportunity to write to someone describing yourself without that person actually having the chance to judge you. An example of this would be my "Letter To My Son" piece. You can start on the following page.

Dear

Salvin Chahal

.

# Elementary

If I went back in time to meet the person I
was in 6<sup>th</sup> grade

.

# Last Time

The last time I cried

.

# Advice

I want you to write down on the left side of
this page different types of advice people
have given you. They can range from
relationships to study habits. Anything that
comes to mind I want you to write it down. On
the right side of this page, write down some
examples of advice you have given other
people. Remember, to keep writing until you
cant. After you have done that, I want you to
circle 3 pieces of advice from the left side and
the right side. So basically you will have 6
pieces of advice in total. Write down why you
selected these specific pieces of advice on the
following page. After that, I want you to write
about the time you went against the advice
you would usually give someone else.

.

.

# Today

Today

.

# Conversation

I asked someone once what made life worth living. That person said, conversation. We go through our lives and have engaging conversations with numerous people. But sometimes, we just want to have a conversation with someone who understands where we are coming from. We start to ask ourselves if that's too much to ask. On the following page I want you to write down a conversation(s) that you'll never forget, changed your life in someway, etc.

# Role Models

Write down a list of people who you consider as "role models." Write down a maximum of 5, and a minimum of 3. After that, write down characteristics of your role models, and why you appreciate those characteristics. But, you have to write down the characteristics and why you appreciate them as if you were writing ingredients for a specific dish.

# Math

My math teachers would always tell me how important math is. I honestly didn't care how long it would take Michael to drive to Dakota, or the area of some random triangle. The only math I understood growing up was the openings. We have 2 openings for our ability to see. We have 2 openings for our ability to hear. We have 2 openings for our ability to smell. But we have only one 1 opening for our ability to speak. 2 obviously becomes before 1 so the only math I knew growing up was to shut up and use the rest of my head before I spoke. On the next page, I want you to start writing about the time you regretted saying something. Even if it was supposed to be said, whatever it may be I want you to write about it.

·

# Home

    I want you to describe to me what types of environments make you happy and why on the left side of this page. On the right side of this page, I want you to write down the type of environments where it's hard to maintain positivity and balance and why. On the following page, I want you to use at least 3 environments from both sides to write about what you would describe as your perfect home.

.

.

# If You

If money wasn't controlling our society like it is now, and you had the ability to do anything you wanted to do, what would you do? If you wanted to buy land for a farm, and get supplies and obtain some animals, it wouldn't cost you anything, and you had the ability to learn whatever you wanted to. What would you do with your life?

.

# About The Author

Salvin Chahal is a poet/emcee from Sacramento, California. He has performed at many venues, festivals and conferences for various audiences. A tangible voice for Generation Y, Chahal's intense delivery and raw self-exploration through rhyme makes him a relatable voice to crowds all around the world. Chahal is a poet mentor and a 2012 SAYS Slam team champion who also works with the community, specifically the youth to emphasize social change and expression through various art forms.

Made in the USA
Charleston, SC
09 January 2015